CODY FIREARMS MUSEUM

Herbert G. Houze

Acknowledgements

Copyright ©1991 by the Buffalo Bill Historical Center

ISBN 0-931618-33-9

Produced by Sequoia Communications
Photography by Devendra Shrikhande and Bob Weiglein
Designed by Brooks Branch
Printed and bound in Thailand

We would like to acknowledge the important efforts of Herbert Houze, former curator of the Cody Firearms Museum, for providing the organizational inspiration and text for this volume. Special thanks are due also to Cameron Laughlin for seeing the project to completion, Frances Clymer who served as editor for the project, Devendra Shrikhande for his photography work, and Gael Oswalt for typing the manuscript.

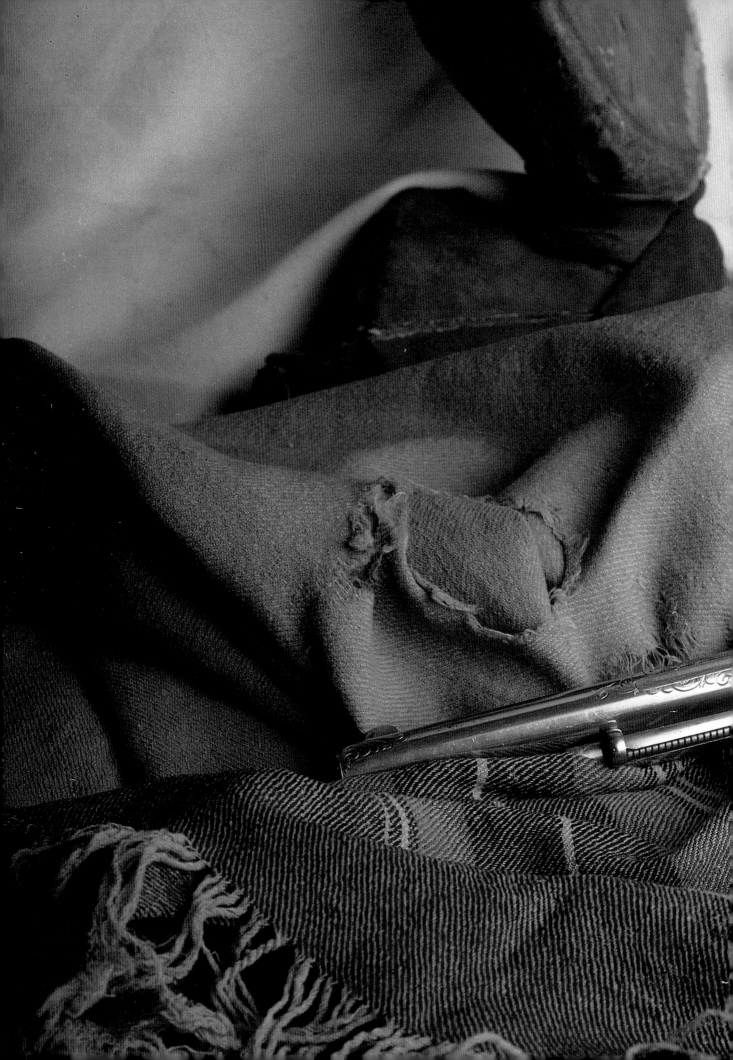

CONTENTS

Introduction

By Peter H. Hassrick

While the name Cody Firearms Museum may bring to mind thoughts of a small, local museum dedicated to firearms used by William F. Cody, nothing could be further from the truth. The Cody Firearms Museum, located in Cody, Wyoming, is, in fact, the largest and most important collection of American and European firearms to be found anywhere. Its nearly five thousand pieces chronicle the development of firearms from their earliest sixteenth-century incarnations to their most modern forms. Even the most common pieces were often decorated in some manner, and the development of this decoration from its humble beginnings to its most elaborate variations can also be traced in the museum's exhibits. Using vintage machinery and replications of two gun shops and a factory, the museum also documents the roles that American arms makers had in the industrialization of the United States.

For many visitors, however, the most important element of the museum is its unparalleled collection of Winchester firearms, which encompasses not only prototypes but also familiar production models. Complementing these are equally important company collections chronicling the work of Colt, Marlin, Parker, Remington, Sharps, and Spencer, as well as other major American firms. Finally, the museum's research collection should not be overlooked. Thousands of nineteenth and early twentieth century engineering and design drawings have been preserved here, together with incomparable assemblages of advertising material and production records. The research collection also includes the personal records of Rudolf J. Kornbrath, one of America's foremost firearm engravers of the early twentieth century.

The Winchester Arms Collection, which is the heart of the Cody Firearms Museum holdings, came to the Buffalo Bill Historical Center in Cody in November 1975, on permanent loan from the Winchester Group of Olin Corporation. It was displayed temporarily in the back third of the Buffalo Bill Museum. In 1981, the collection moved to new quarters in a 15,000-square-foot gallery directly below the Buffalo Bill Museum. In that location, it was referred to as the Winchester Arms Museum. In 1988, as part of a plan to physically expand that facility, the Olin Corporation transferred full title to the collection to the Historical Center, the single most impressive and magnanimous gift in the museum's history. A new wing to house the collection was opened in 1991 and dedicated as the Cody Firearms Museum.

This catalog was prepared for that occasion. We would like to thank the major donors who made this new museum possible. They include the estate of Ernest J. Goppert, the Robert W. Woodruff Foundation, Inc., Sturm, Ruger and Company, the National Endowment for the Humanities, the Kresge Foundation, the Val A. Browning Foundation, the Boone and Crockett Club, Spencer T. and Ann W. Olin Foundation, William D. Weiss, Silas S. Cathcart, the Olin Corporation Charitable Trust, and the John M. Olin Foundation.

The eighty-eight pieces shown in this catalog are only a fraction of the many firearms to be found in the collection of the Cody Firearms Museum. It is hoped that they will provide you an inspiring glimpse of what has been called the finest collection of firearms in the world.

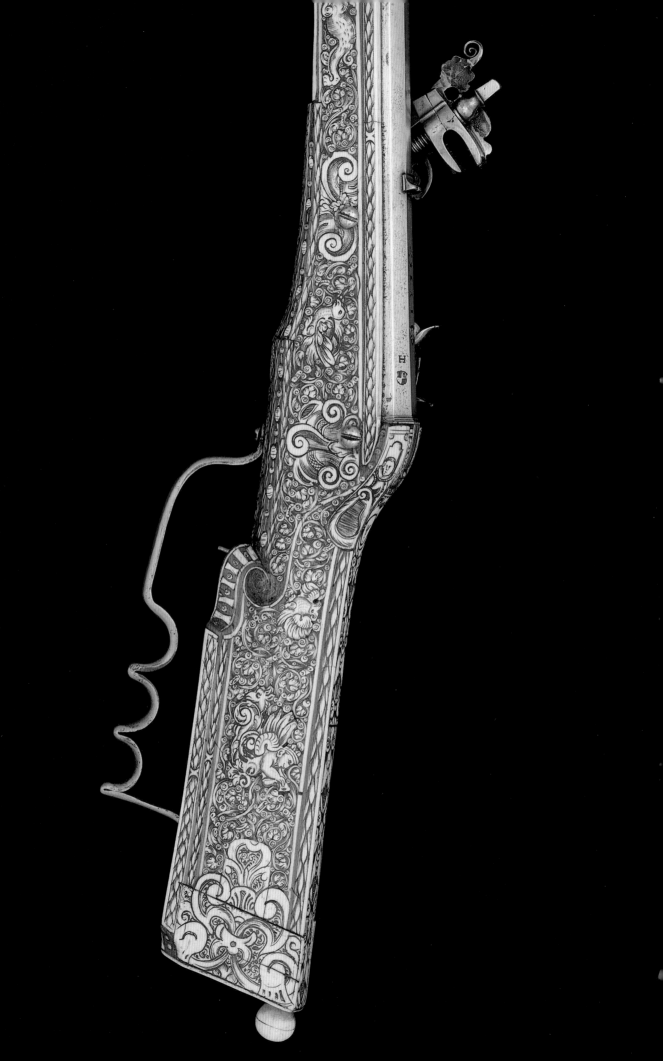

Early Firearms

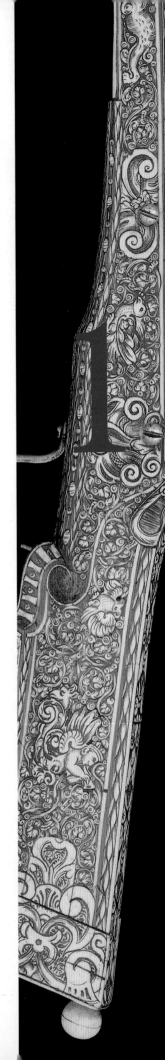

A lthough the use of cannon in Europe can be documented as early as 1326, the appearance of hand-held firearms is set a few decades later, in the 1340s. In their earliest forms, firearms were little more than iron or bronze tubes plugged at one end and pierced with a vent hole to which a match or hot poker could be put. The stocks fitted to these early weapons were simple, straight wooden or metal extensions that could be held under the armpit.

The major disadvantages of early firearms were their weight and the inconsistency of the metal used in casting. All too often, barrels would burst due to excessive loading with black powder or to flaws in the casting of the barrels themselves. An excellent example of the danger of casting flaws can be seen in the section of a fifteenth century wall gun breech, found in the ruins of Castle Niedeck near Weinheim, Germany. Improper casting of the barrel resulted in a number of internal bubbles that so weakened the gun that it burst when fired—probably with disastrous results for the shooter.

By the beginning of the sixteenth century, improvements in the manufacture of iron and bronze made it possible to create truly portable firearms. Initially, only the military used them. However, by 1530 arms for sporting purposes had appeared. The most common method of firing these early arms was by using a treated cord or match to ignite a small amount of fine priming powder in a pan at the breech vent. The matchlock muskets required hunters to stand still while shooting game animals and birds. Their use was also governed by the weather, since strong winds could blow the priming powder out of the pan attached to the barrel breech, and rain could either extinguish the match or make the priming powder too wet to be useable. To counteract these deficiencies, early gunmakers began to look for other methods of firing.

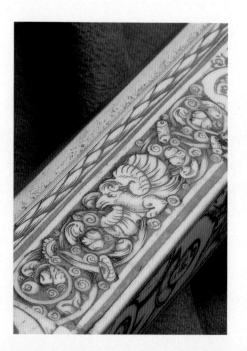

One of the first ignition systems to be developed was the wheel lock, whose action may be likened to that of a modern cigarette lighter. A spring-wound circular wheel with notches cut in its edge mounted vertically into a lock plate, so that when the trigger was pulled it rotated at high speed. When the cock holding iron pyrites was lowered so that the pyrites pressed against the wheel, the latter's rotation produced a shower of sparks, thereby igniting the priming powder. To keep the priming powder dry until the moment of firing, the pan was fitted with a sliding cover that could be either manually or automatically opened when the arm was fired. The development

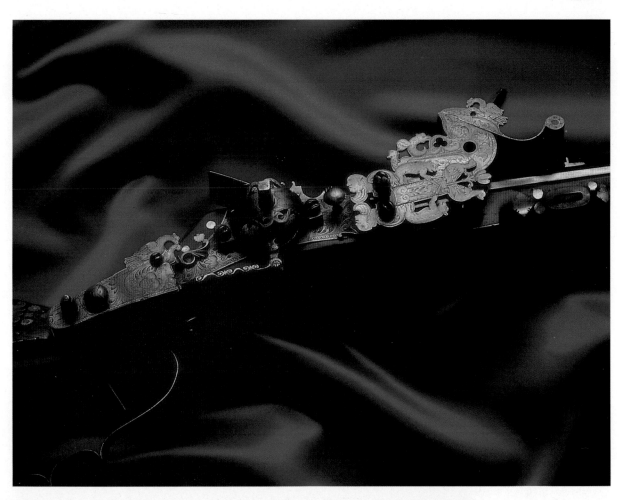

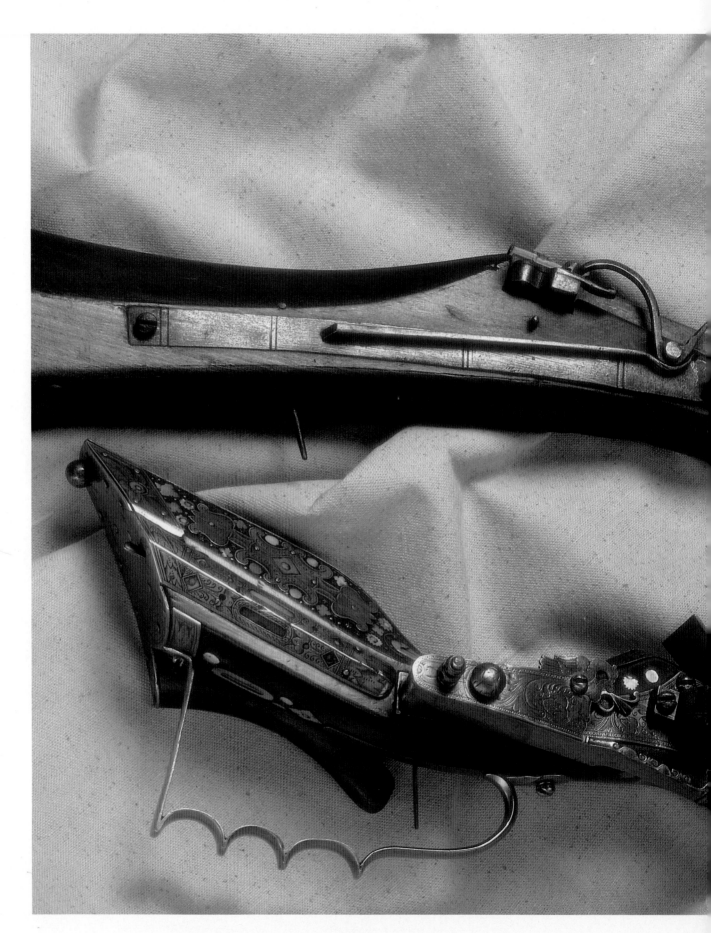

of the wheel lock enabled the manufacture of truly effective pistols—a fact that alarmed many European rulers and resulted in the issuance of laws limiting or prohibiting their use. Despite the obvious advantages of this system over its predecessor, the cost of its manufacture prohibited its general use. Some European armies thus continued to issue matchlock muskets well after they had been rendered obsolete.

In America, archaeological recoveries at the site of the Jamestown, Virginia, settlement indicate that matchlock firearms were widely used in America during the early 1600s. Eventually, as in Europe, the more efficient flintlock replaced the matchlock.

The end of the sixteenth century saw the development of another ignition system that used pyrites and steel: the snaphaunce lock. In this system, the cock holding the pyrites was not manually lowered, but instead snapped forward under spring tension when the trigger was pulled. As it snapped forward, the pyrites struck a steel that pivoted on a pin inserted in the lock plate, and sparks fell into the automatically opened priming pan. The incorporation of the automatic pan cover made this new system almost waterproof. By the 1630s, this lock had been further perfected by making the base of the steel in such a way that it covered the priming pan itself. This new design, known as the flintlock, became the dominant form of firearms ignition for almost the next two centuries.

Powder Horns and Flasks

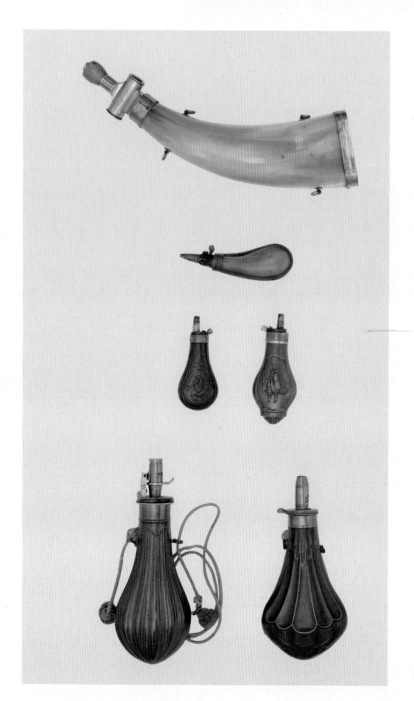

The adage "Keep Your Powder Dry" was not an idle statement prior to the introduction of metallic cartridges. Preventing moisture from contaminating powder could mean the difference between obtaining game to eat and going hungry, or, in the worst case, between life and death.

From the sixteenth to nineteenth centuries, one of the most popular means of keeping powder dry was to use containers of bone or horn fitted with spring-loaded stoppers or wooden plugs. While often plain, powder flasks and horns could be decorated with engraved or carved ornaments. Sometimes the decoration only involved marking the horn or flask with the owner's name, but often it was more sophisticated. Indeed, highly decorated flasks made of ivory, silver, or gilded metal were supplied with luxury arms. During the French and Indian Wars as well as during the American Revolution, soldiers inscribed their powder horns with patriotic motifs and sayings. Some horns from this period displayed the major river routes in North America and points of reference along those rivers, so that they could do double-duty as road maps.

During the nineteenth century, pressed copper flasks became the common means to store and carry powder. Flasks of this type were embossed with all manner of decoration, from portraits of George Washington to scenes of the hunt.

With the introduction of metallic cartridges, however, the need for powder flasks and horns diminished rapidly. By the turn of this century they had become curiosities instead of indispensable tools—more likely to be hung on a wall as decoration than to be suspended from a hunter's belt.

Engraving

From the very beginning of firearms manufacture, gunmakers as well as owners have tried to personalize pieces by means of decoration. Whether this decoration took the form of simple carving or elaborate gold inlays, the goal was to create a piece that could be easily distinguished from others of the same type.

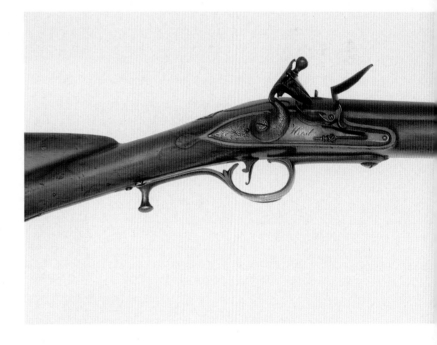

A survey of arms decoration demonstrates that it has for the most part followed the prevailing styles and fashions of the decorative arts through the past five centuries. Artists' engraving patterns, strictly for use on firearms, incorporated elements found in the decoration of furniture, porcelain, silver, and so forth. Arms decoration also reflected the regions in which firearms were made. Inasmuch as this work was carried out in steel, the determination and skill of the engravers are admirable—especially in those instances where the metal was cut away to create sculptural effects.

During the past century and a half, however, arms decoration has remained somewhat more universal and constant in nature. Those exceptions that do exist represent a continuation of a tradition that is almost as old as gunmaking itself.

Hand Cannon Breech Section
German
Circa 1450-1500
Overall length: 4¾″
This fragment of a hand cannon graphically demonstrates one of the problems encountered in early firearms: faulty casting. The interior view of the piece illustrates that numerous air bubbles remained in the metal when it was cast. As a result, the breech blew apart when the gun was fired—evidently after little use, as the pan displays little wear.

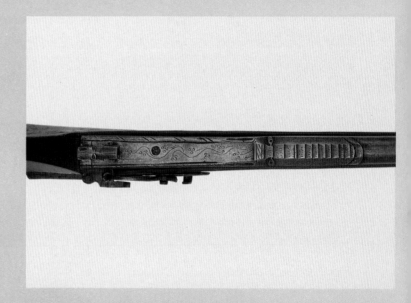

Matchlock Fowler
Swiss
Circa 1540-1550
Maker unidentified
Overall length: 45¼″
Barrel length: 35½″
Caliber: .51
Although almost identical in form to military muskets of the same period, the decoration and light weight of this gun indicate that it was probably made for sporting purposes. The barrel is carved at the muzzle and breech with a stylized representation of a bearded man.

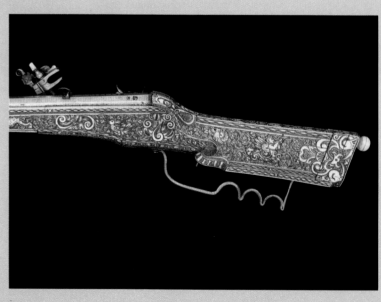

Wheel Lock Carbine
South German
1596
Signed: Monogrammist HG
Overall length: 35½″
Barrel length: 24¼″
Caliber: .40
The presence of the arms of Saxony and those of the Archmarshalship of the Holy Roman Empire, engraved on the gilt wheel cover, indicates that this carbine was made for Grand Duke Christian II, Elector of Saxony. The stock is intricately inlaid with bone, ivory scrolls, and pellets surrounding Renaissance figural representations.

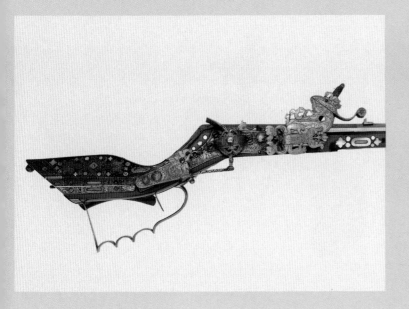

Wheel Lock Rifle
Silesian
Circa 1650
Unsigned
Overall length: 47″
Barrel length: 37″
Caliber: .36
Wheel lock rifles of this form are peculiar to Silesia, a region of southwestern Poland and a small part of Czechoslovakia and eastern Germany, and are known as Tschinkes. Although awkward looking, they are extremely well-balanced, as well as light in weight. The decorative motifs to be found on arms of this type owe their origin to Polish and Russian art.

◀

Miquelet Blunderbuss
Italian
Circa 1680
Signed: Lazarino Cominazzo
Overall length: 29½″
Barrel length: 16⅝″
Caliber: 1.75
The miquelet lock with its exposed mainspring was a variation of the flintlock, popular in Spain and Italy. The hinged buttstock allowed the arm to be folded into a more compact form for carrying in a coach or under a cape. The flared muzzle of blunderbuss-type firearms was made in the mistaken belief that the shot or bullets which with they were loaded would disperse immediately in front of the muzzle, thus increasing the weapon's effectiveness.

◀

Flintlock Pistol Carbine
Flemish
Circa 1640-1650
Signed: Monogrammist W
Overall length: 34″
Barrel length: 27⅝″
Caliber: .42
Gift of H.G. Houze
This pistol was designed for boar-hunting from horseback, and was originally fitted with an extension that incorporated a knife. As befits its original purpose, the grip is realistically carved in the shape of a boar being attacked by hounds.

▶

Flintlock Pistol
German
Circa 1710
Signed: Weber, Berlin
Overall length: 5⅞″
Barrel length: 2¾″
Caliber: .33
Made well over one hundred years prior to the percussion pocket pistols popularized by Henry Deringer, this little pistol is an excellent example of earlier forms of personal sidearms.

▲

Breech-Loading Flintlock Pistol
English
Circa 1720
Signed: H. Delany, London
Overall length: 11¾″
Barrel length: 5⅛″
Caliber: .62
One of the most popular breech-loading firearms made during the seventeenth and eighteenth centuries was the turn-off pistol. To load, the barrel was unscrewed and the charge of powder and ball were placed directly in the breech. When the barrel was screwed back on, the arm could be primed and fired.

▲

Flintlock Blunderbuss
Russian
Circa 1750
Made at the Tula Arsenal
Overall length: 35⅜″
Barrel length: 19¾″
Caliber: 1⅞
The barrel of this arm is inlaid, in two colors of gold,
with the Royal Arms of France as well as iconographic
details representative of France, such as the cock. The
silver medallion forward of the breech is sculpted with
a portrait believed to be of Louis XV. By tradition, this
blunderbuss formed part of a garniture, or set of fire-
arms, presented by the Empress Elizabeth of Russia to
King Louis XV of France.

◀

Flintlock Pistols
Austrian
Circa 1750
Unsigned
Overall length: 16″
Barrel length: 10¼″
Caliber: .58
The form and decoration of these holster pistols are
typical of work produced in Austria during the eighteenth
century. The use of brass for the mounts (buttcap,
trigger guard, etc.), as well as for inlay work on the
barrel is especially striking against the fruitwood stock.

▶

Breech-Loading Flintlock Rifle
English
Circa 1762
Signed: Hirst, London
Overall length: 49½"
Barrel length: 34"
Caliber: .79

In an attempt to simplify loading, rifles such as this
one were made with trigger guards that had at their
forward end a threaded plug that, when unscrewed,
allowed access to the barrel breech. To load the gun,
the trigger guard was turned several times to unscrew
the plug, a ball was then inserted into the bore, and
allowed to roll forward until held by the rifling. A set
amount of powder was poured into the breech and the
plug was reinserted. After the pan located on the lock
was primed, the rifle was ready for firing. The presence
of English Board of Ordnance proof marks on the barrel
may indicate that this rifle is one of the five produced
for the testing of the breech-loading system by the
Board of Ordnance in 1762.

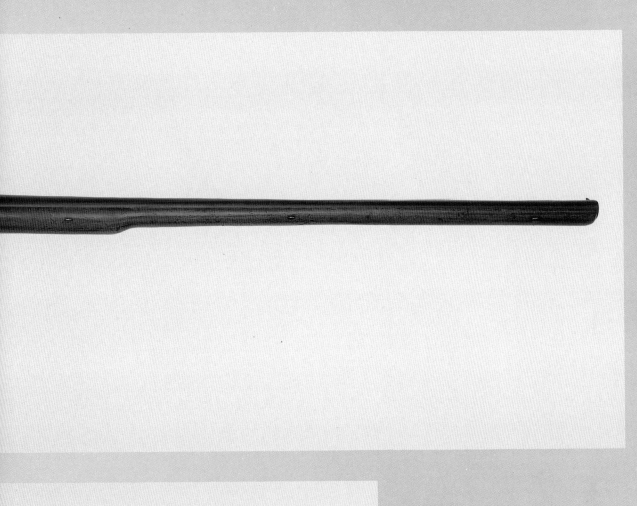

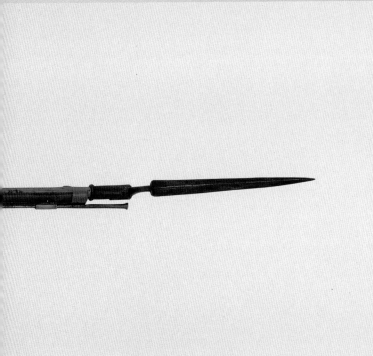

Flintlock Musket
German
Circa 1770
Unsigned
Overall length: 57⅛″
Barrel length: 42½″
Caliber: .79
Captured at the Battle of Trenton in 1776, this musket
is typical of those carried by Hessian mercenaries
during the American Revolution.

Early American Firearms

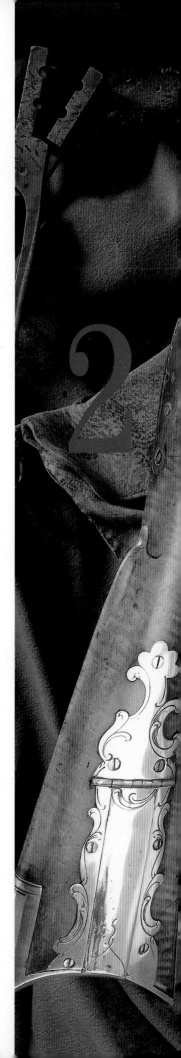

In colonial America, firearms played an important role in the establishment of settlements and the gradual westward expansion of the population. Apart from being tools for defense, firearms were essential to early settlers' survival. Smooth bore longarms supplied small game and wild fowl for the table and, when the need arose, could be used as muskets for military duty. Though these plain, workmanlike weapons were the mainstay of the colonists' arsenal, they have been more or less consigned to historical obscurity. The flintlock that seems to epitomize that era is the Pennsylvania rifle—also popularly called the Kentucky rifle, due to its widespread use in that state. Developed from German prototypes during the eighteenth century, the Pennsylvania rifle is characterized by long, graceful lines. The use of maple for the stock and brass for the mounts created an aesthetically pleasing impression. To a great extent, Pennsylvania rifles gave rise to the romance of American firearms, for their peculiarities and characteristics resulted in their being given names like "Old Betsy" and "Sure Shot." This personalization by their original owners passed into the folklore of the nation. To this day, the mention of such names calls to mind a long, handsome rifle in the hands of a buckskin-clad frontiersman.

The role that firearms such as the Pennsylvania rifle played in the spread of firearm ornamentation should not be underestimated. A rifle made in Bucks County, Pennsylvania, displaying the form and combination of engraved or carved C scrolls particular to that region, could have been carried into Ohio, or even further where another gunmaker might take inspiration from its decoration for use in his own pieces. The existence of some pieces of furniture decorated with carving typical of that found on firearms made in faraway locales certainly suggests that arms played an important role in the spread of artistic styles.

After the Revolutionary War (1775-1783), gunmakers in all parts of the fledgling American republic flourished. The increasing size of the middle class also gave rise to a greater demand for high-quality sporting and target firearms. In Europe, the demand for engraved and inlaid luxury arms remained constant throughout the period of the flintlock's use. In England, the technical improvement of firearms received more emphasis than their decoration, while firearms produced on the Continent often exhibited an exuberant attention to appearance. The work of Nicholas Noël Boutet, artistic director of the French National Arms Factory at Versailles, perhaps best exemplified this trend. The presentation rifles, shotguns, pistols, and swords manufactured there embodied all of the traits of the neo-classical style popular with the court of Napoleon I. A reaction to the flamboyance of the rococo style in vogue before the French Revolution of 1789, neo-classicism is characterized by a restrained elegance that drew its inspiration from the art of the Roman Empire and Egypt. It is fitting that the era of the flintlock came to an end with a flourish rather than a whimper.

Women and Firearms

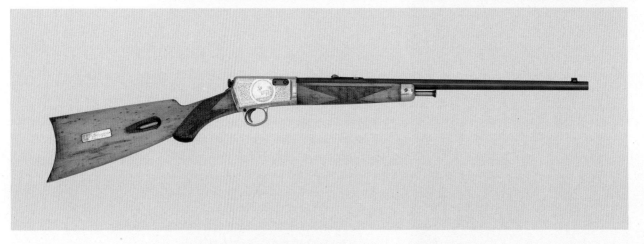

BUFFALO BILL'S WILD WEST
CONGRESS, ROUGH RIDERS OF THE WORLD.

MISS ANNIE OAKLEY,
THE PEERLESS LADY WING-SHOT.

Among history's legendary trick and exhibition shooters, Annie Oakley— "The Peerless Lady Wing-Shot"— comes readily to mind. Despite current notions, Annie Oakley was not a unique personage; rather, she was just one of the more famous woman shooters.

History and folklore abound with stories of how determined women defended their frontier homes or put meat on the table for their families. From Catherine the Great of Russia to Olympic hopefuls of today, women have always participated in shooting sports, often with better results than men. Although this fact is often overlooked by the public in general, the firearms industry has always encouraged female participation in what is commonly perceived as a masculine avocation. Lighter weight firearms have been produced from the sixteenth century to today for specific use by women.

Whether their firearms have been light or heavy, however, women from every station in life have used firearms for defense, the hunt, and sport across the centuries. To no less extent than men, women's use of firearms should be recognized and appreciated.

Children
and Firearms

Training children in the use and care of
firearms is a centuries-old family tradition
in many cultures—a heritage reflected in
the smaller weapons produced for youths since
the Renaissance.

One of the most famous children with well-
documented expertise in firearms was King
Louis XIII of France, who was born in 1601. His
biographers recorded that he began collecting
arms prior to age ten and was proficient in their
use and construction by the time he reached
thirteen. Indeed, it is noted that one of his
favorite diversions was to take apart and
clean the arms in his collection.

On a more common level, during the eighteenth
and nineteenth centuries, children were routinely
trained in how to use the family rifle or shotgun.
Not only did this provide some element of added
protection for households, but it also meant that
youths could be sent forth to secure small game
for the table.

Among wealthy families, some lucky children had
reduced-scale firearms made for them. Apart from
their smaller size, these pieces were in all
respects identical to their larger counterparts.

During the twentieth century, children have
a culturally acceptable opportunity to learn
firearms use and safety within the contexts
of target shooting and hunter safety classes.

▶
Flintlock Musket
American
Circa 1776
Unsigned
Overall length: 57⅜″
Barrel length: 41¾″
Caliber: .80
At the beginning of the American Revolution in 1775,
a number of local gunsmiths were pressed into service
to produce military arms for state troops. Those arms,
which followed the form of the Long Land flintlock
musket carried by British troops, saw heavy service
during the war and even afterward, when many were
used for sporting purposes.

▶
Flintlock Rifle
American
Circa 1800
Signed: N. Beyer
Overall length: 58¾″
Barrel length: 42¾″
Caliber: .52
The Pennsylvania rifle is perhaps the most widely
recognized firearm to have been manufactured in the
United States. Combining grace and accuracy, rifles
of this type are acknowledged to be the finest products
of early American gunsmiths.

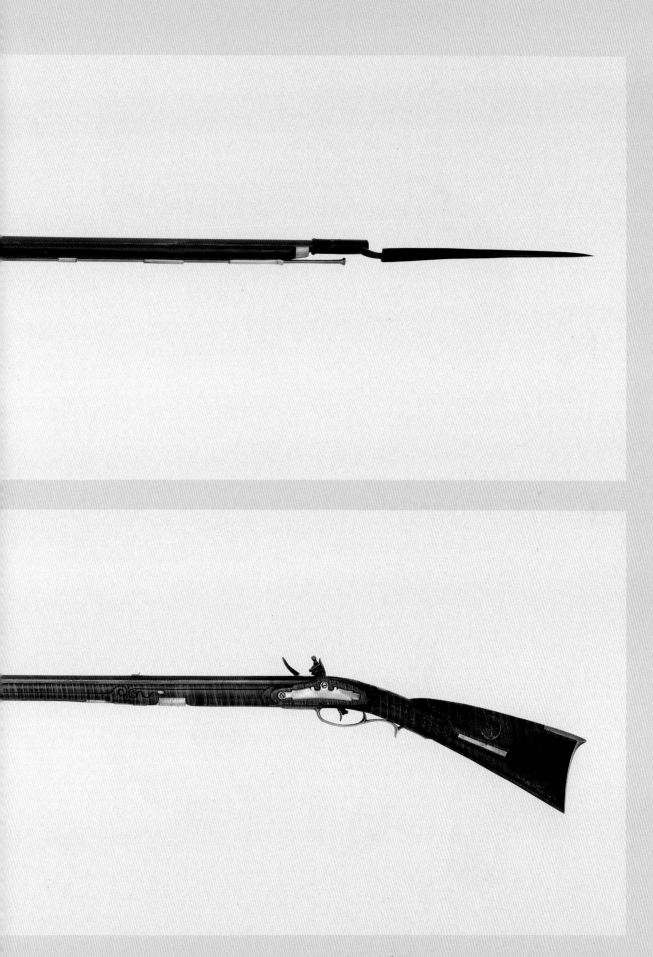

▲
Flintlock Pistol
American
Circa 1790-1800
Signed: Bielby & Company, Colchester, Connecticut
Overall length: 13½"
Barrel length: 8¾"
Caliber: .48
This silver-mounted, brass-barreled pistol is typical
of many arms produced at the turn of the nineteenth
century for use in America.

▼
Flintlock Pistol
English
Circa 1800
Signed: Goodwin & Company, London, England
Overall length: 8¾"
Barrel length: 2½"
Caliber: .50
Designed for use by naval officers, "Duck's Foot" pistols
were particularly effective in quelling mutinies or repel-
ling boarders, as all four barrels fired simultaneously.

▲
Flintlock Pistols
French
Circa 1820
Signed: Boutet Versailles
Overall length: 13¼"
Barrel length: 7¼"
Caliber: .58
Loaned by Willis McDonald IV
One of the most famous nineteenth-century French
gunsmiths was Nicholas Noël Boutet who produced
large numbers of plain and highly decorated arms
for the court of Napoleon I. Although dating from
the period after the restoration of the French
monarchy and Boutet's fall from favor, these
pistols still embody many of the characteristics
for which he was justifiably famous.

The Percussion Era

The "Percussion Era" owes its origin to the work of a Scottish minister, the Reverend Alexander Forsyth, who was an avid sportsman. Like many well-educated men of the late eighteenth and early nineteenth centuries who were heirs to the intellectual and philosophical legacy of the Enlightenment, the Reverend Forsyth was deeply interested in the natural sciences. In 1805, he began experiments to explore the use of fulminates of mercury or silver as ignition agents for gunpowder. Past experiments had demonstrated that fulminate of mercury crystals exploded violently when hit, but Forsyth invented a process by which this force could be controlled for use in gunlocks. The lock he patented in 1807 contained a revolving priming magazine that held a small supply of fulminate of mercury pellets. When the magazine was rotated upward, one pellet would fall into a cut in the axis arbor. When the magazine returned to its normal position, this pellet lay directly below a springloaded striker housed in the upper part of the magazine. The action of the falling hammer thus caused the striker to hit the priming pellet and fire the main charge. As a safety precaution, in case the pellets in the magazine accidently exploded, the base of the pellet reservoir was fitted with a cork plug that could blow out without causing damage.

After the expiration of Forsyth's patent years later, various other inventions harnessed the power of fulminate of mercury. The most common of these devices, devised in the 1820s, was a small copper cap that had a pellet placed on the upper inside surface. When placed over a hollow nipple, the explosion of the cap was transmitted directly into the gun barrel. Despite the obvious advantages of this new system, such as simplicity and water proofing, many gun users retained allegiance to the flintlock. As late as 1840, the United States government planned to issue flintlock muskets for infantry use.

The success of the percussion cap enabled the rapid development of repeating firearms. While attempts to devise repeating firearms had been made from the sixteenth century on, their invention became practicable only with the introduction of the percussion ignition system. The most popular designs were the "pepperbox" (or "pepperpot"), which had a group of revolving barrels, and the true revolver, which had a separate cylinder that rotated when either the trigger was pulled or the hammer was cocked. Of the last type, the revolver designed by Samuel Colt in 1836 achieved the greatest fame; in fact, the name Colt became synonymous with the word revolver. During the California Gold Rush (1848-

1850), New York outfitters advised prospective miners that a pair of Colt revolvers was a necessary addition to their equipment.

The introduction of the revolver also coincided with the industrialization of American arms manufacturing. Cotton gin inventor Eli Whitney had devised the first standard, interchangeable gun parts around the turn of the century, and these standardized parts could now be made by fixed machinery. Their first large-scale manufacture took place at Samuel Colt's factory in Hartford, Connecticut; by 1850, gunmaking in America had ceased to be a one-man cottage industry (except for some specialty gunsmiths). With the outbreak of the Civil War a year later, firearm industrialization shifted into high gear, and efforts began to develop firearms that used self-contained metallic cartridges.

An unfortunate byproduct of the mass production of firearms was the loss of each gun's individually crafted identity. No longer were they unique and personalized possessions; instead, they became merely useful objects. This, coupled with the increasing urbanization of a society that, at least in the East, no longer defended its households with guns or shot its own game every day for dinner, brought about a new, negative perception of firearms. In the West, however, firearms remained essential tools for survival, and were still accepted and appreciated as a part of life.

Locks

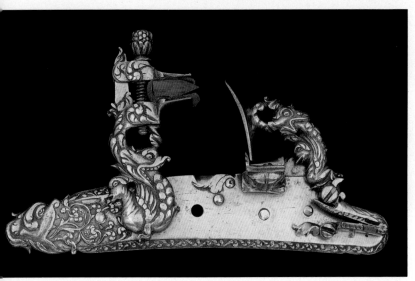

Often, when one looks at a firearm, it is easy to overlook small details in favor of the whole. This is especially true of highly decorated arms that boast intricately carved or inlaid stocks, or engraved or otherwise embellished locks and barrels. Even in plain arms, the tendency is to appreciate the whole rather than individual elements.

Prior to the industrialization of the arms industry, gunmakers routinely lavished their considerable skills on the locks of firearms. The importance of the lock lay in the fact that if it were not properly made, arms would not function.

Apart from ensuring the locks' technical operation, gunmakers often polished and engraved interior surfaces and parts that were normally hidden from view. Though this practice diminished as time passed, it was never totally abandoned. Even in the nineteenth century, the interior parts and surfaces of the best gun locks were made and polished with a precision comparable to that practiced by watchmakers.

American Indians and Firearms

Perhaps one of the most common images of the American West is that of an American Indian on horseback, carrying a Winchester rifle. While the film industry has stereotyped this image, it is, in fact, based upon truth.

From the first moment of colonization, the settlers exchanged firearms with Native Americans to obtain food and furs, and to seal peace treaties. Recent research demonstrates that the Native Americans from the seventeenth century forward sought out the most modern arms available and tried to secure them whenever possible.

The firearms most circulated among native tribes were the trade muskets produced for the Hudson Bay and Northwest Fur Companies. These long, ungainly weapons were usually cut down by their Indian owners to make them more portable.

During the nineteenth century, Native Americans of the western tribes used whatever arms they could get, and after the Civil War, they were among the first to appreciate the capabilities of repeating rifles such as the Winchester.

Indian-owned arms, with their brass tack decoration and worn parts, graphically evoke the era of their use.

Percussion Rifle
American
Circa 1815
Signed: J. Coe
Overall length: 52¼″
Barrel length: 36″
Caliber: .43
The value of the percussion ignition system spread
rapidly in the United States soon after its development
in England. This Pennsylvania-style rifle, adapted to
fire by means of fulminate of mercury pellets, is typical
of many arms made between 1810 and 1820. The lock
form, however, did not complement the graceful lines
of arms developed for use with flintlock side locks.

▶

Percussion Revolver
American
Circa 1838
Signed: Patent Arms Manufacturing Company,
Paterson, New Jersey
Overall length: 8″
Barrel length: 4½″
Caliber: .33
The revolver designed by Samuel Colt, protected by
his patent of February 25, 1836, was first produced
in Paterson, New Jersey. Although fragile in many
respects and rather expensive for the era, Colt's patent
revolvers were immediately recognized as the coming
gun. While the Paterson venture proved to be a financial
failure, Colt's next attempt to mass-produce firearms
was an unqualified success.

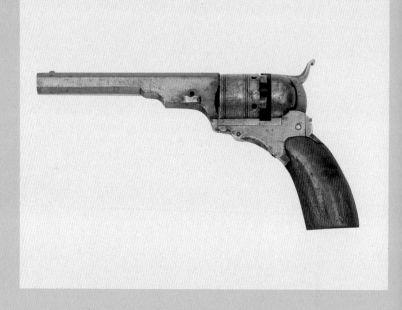

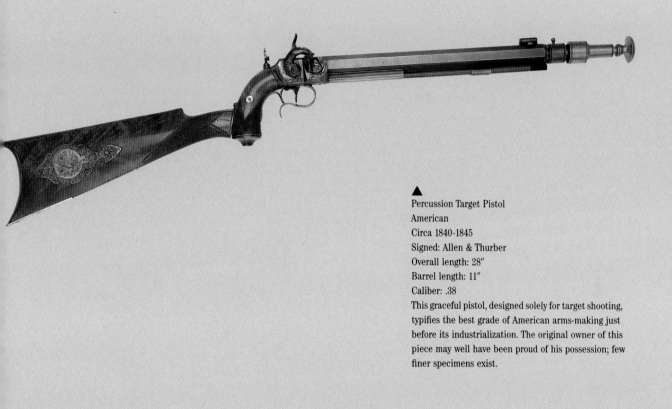

▲
Percussion Target Pistol
American
Circa 1840-1845
Signed: Allen & Thurber
Overall length: 28″
Barrel length: 11″
Caliber: .38
This graceful pistol, designed solely for target shooting,
typifies the best grade of American arms-making just
before its industrialization. The original owner of this
piece may well have been proud of his possession; few
finer specimens exist.

▲
Percussion Pepperbox Rifle
American
Circa 1845
Signed: W.M. Briggs, Potsdam, New York
Overall length: 38″
Barrel length: 21¼″
Caliber: .35
While the pepperbox's revolving group of barrels
was extremely popular in handgun form, it is rarely
encountered in longarms, due to the excessive weight
of the barrels. Although this example weighs ten pounds
and fourteen ounces, its form allowed the production
of a balanced arm. The decoration of the stock with
engraved silver mounts is typical of the best quality
work produced by local gunsmiths during the first half
of the nineteenth century.

▲

Percussion Pepperbox Revolver
American
Circa 1845-185
Signed: Allen & Thurber
Overall length: 7½″
Barrel length: 3¼″
Caliber: .32
The pepperbox is identifiable by its use of a rotating
group of barrels machined from a solid block of iron.
Although heavier than revolvers of conventional
construction, the pepperbox was highly favored during
the 1840s and 1850s, especially among those traveling
and working in Californian gold fields.

▲
Percussion Revolving Rifle
Belgian
Circa 1855
Unsigned
Overall length: 38½″
Barrel length: 21½″
Caliber: .36
Patterned directly after the American Wesson & Leavitt
revolvers, this rifle is distinguishable as a Belgian
product only because of the European trigger guard
style, the form of the engraving, and the presence of
Liège proofmarks. Within ten years after this arm was
made, the engraved ornament on the lockplate would
have been barely different from that found on American
sporting arms.

▲
Percussion Revolver
American
Circa 1850
Maker: Wesson & Leavitt
Overall length: 10½″
Barrel length: 4¾″
Caliber: .31
Produced to compete with the Colt revolver, the Wesson
& Leavitt design never achieved wide popularity.
Despite this, it is interesting to note that some foreign
gunmakers copied the design.

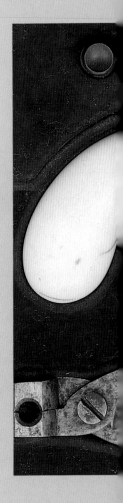

►
Percussion Pistols
French
Circa 1850
Unsigned
Overall length: 4¼″
Barrel length: 1⅜″
Caliber: .31
During the mid-nineteenth century it was fashionable
for European ladies to carry small pistols for protec-
tion. Commonly referred to as muff pistols, since they
were easily concealed in handmuffs during colder
months, pistols of this type are characterized by
their diminutive size, folding triggers (which auto-
matically pop down when the hammer is cocked),
and turn-off barrels.

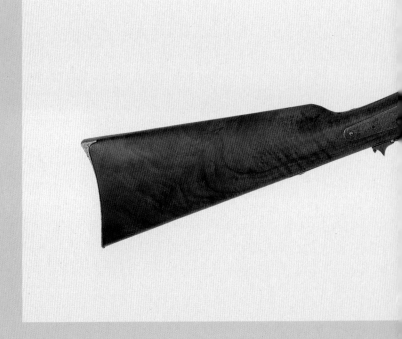

►
Breech-Loading Percussion Shotgun
American
Circa 1855
Maker: Sharps Rifle Company, Hartford, Connecticut
Overall length: 38″
Barrel length: 21″
Gauge: 26
Though best remembered for its rifles, the Sharps
Company did produce a number of fine shotguns.
Between 1854 and 1856 the company made approxi-
mately 320 Model 1853 shotguns.

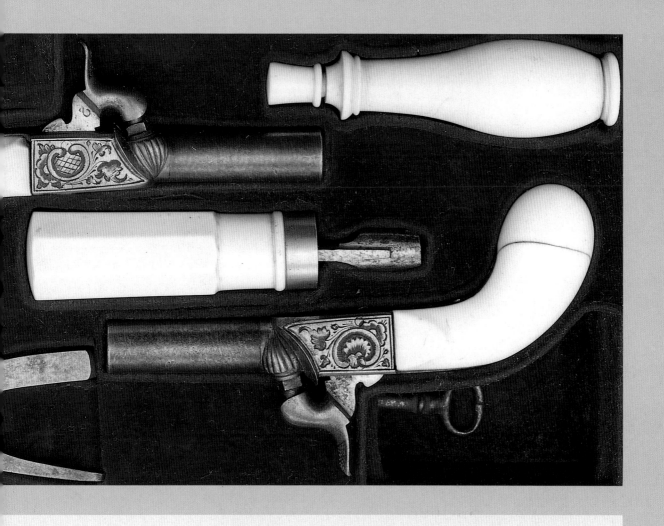

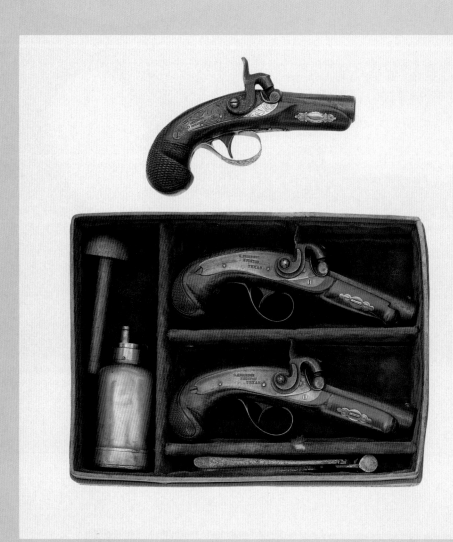

▶

Percussion Revolver
American
Circa 1850-1855
Unsigned
Overall length: 7″
Barrel length: 2¾″
Caliber: .31

▶

Percussion Revolver
American
Circa 1850-1855
Unsigned
Overall length: 7½″
Barrel length: 3¼″
Caliber: .31

▶

Percussion Revolver
American
Circa 1850-1855
Unsigned
Overall length: 8½″
Barrel length: 3⅜″
Caliber: .31

▶

Percussion Revolver
American
Circa 1850-1855
Unsigned
Overall length: 11″
Barrel length: 5¼″
Caliber: .36

▲
Percussion Pistols
American
Circa 1855
Signed: G. Erichson, Houston, Texas
Overall length: 6¼″
Barrel length: 2½″
Caliber: .47
Patterned after the percussion pocket pistols made
famous by Henry Deringer, these pistols demonstrate
that first-rate gunsmiths could be found even on the
edges of the American frontier during the nineteenth
century.

▲
Percussion Pistol
American
Circa 1855
Signed: Henry Deringer, Philadelphia
Overall length: 5⅝″
Barrel length: 2″
Caliber: .44
Among the most widely distributed and copied American
firearms of the nineteenth century, the hand-sized
pocket pistol first developed by Henry Deringer stands
alone. Popular with people from all walks of life, the
Deringer pistol was produced in vast quantities both
in the United States and abroad. The name Deringer
became synonymous with all such pistols.

▲
Percussion Revolver
American
Circa 1850-1855
Unsigned [Blunt & Syms, New York, New York]
Overall length: 5⅝″
Barrel length: 2″
Caliber: .27
This group of pepperbox revolvers illustrates the
diversity in style and size that could be produced by
one manufacturer—in this instance, the New York firm
of Blunt & Syms. From small, easily concealed pocket
pistols to large pieces of a size intended for holster use,
each model met the varied requirements of potential
purchasers from East Coast cities to the California
gold fields.

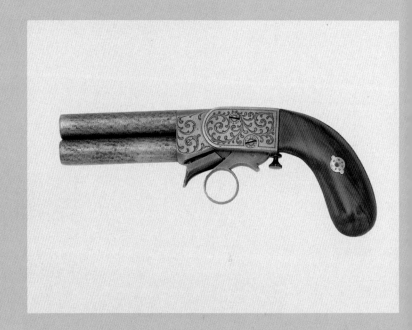

▶
Percussion Volley Pistol
Belgian
Circa 1855
Signed: J. Herman, Liège, Belgium
Overall length: 8⅜″
Barrel length: 3″
Caliber: .48
Both barrels of this pistol can be fired simultaneously
if the nipples are capped. By using one percussion
cap, the pistol can be used as a single shot. The knob
behind the trigger is a safety catch to hold the hammer
at full cock.

◀
Percussion Revolver
American
Circa 1860
Unsigned [B.J. Hart & Brother, New York, New York]
Overall length: 7½″
Barrel length: 3″
Caliber: .35
Among the various revolvers produced by small
manufacturers in direct competition with the Colt,
Remington and Whitney Companies, the double-
action Hart revolver was one of the most aesthetically
pleasing, but shortest lived.

◀
Percussion Rifle
American
Circa 1861-1862
Unsigned [Read and Watson, Wytheville, Virginia]
Overall length: 42½″
Barrel length: 26⅛″
Caliber: .53
After the Confederacy captured the federal armory at
Harpers Ferry, Virginia, large quantities of finished and
partially finished arms components were shipped south
for fabrication into finished weapons. The firm of Read
& Watson in Wytheville, Virginia, used Hall rifle parts to
build a series of muzzle-loading carbines such as this
that were issued to Confederate troops.

▲
Percussion Revolving Rifle and Shotgun
French
Circa 1862
Signed: Colonel LeMat, Paris, France
Overall length: 36½″
Barrel length: 19½″
Caliber: .43/24 gauge
Designed by Colonel Jean Alexandre François LeMat
of New Orleans, Louisiana, this style of arm, which
combined the benefits of a revolver with those of a
shotgun, was made only in England and Europe. Popular
with Confederate soldiers, LeMat carbines and pistols
were extensively imported by the South.

▲
Percussion Revolver
American
Circa 1862-1864
Unsigned
Overall length: 12⅝″
Barrel length: 7″
Caliber: .36
In December of 1862, the firm of Spiller & Burr began
production of revolvers for the Confederate government.
Based on the .36-caliber revolver made by the Whitney
Arms Company, the Spiller & Burr was one of the finest
military sidearms manufactured in the Confederacy. In
order to reduce production problems, the frames of
these revolvers were made of brass, a much more easily
worked metal than steel. By the end of the Civil War,
the Spiller & Burr factory had produced approximately
1,400 revolvers.

▲
Breech-Loading Percussion Rifle
American
Circa 1863
Unsigned [Designed by Hiram Berdan]
Overall length: 55½"
Barrel length: 39"
Caliber: .44
One of the most unusual firearms to have been made during the Civil War, this rifle's hammer is sculpted into a portrait bust of President Abraham Lincoln. The Cody Firearms Museum's collections boast the only known example.

◄
Percussion Target Pistols
French
Circa 1865
Signed: Gastinne Renette
Overall length: 16⅜"
Barrel length: 8¾"
Caliber: .47
Gift of the John M. Olin Estate
This pair of target pistols, typical of those produced in France from 1835 to 1880, was awarded to the Count R. D'Hérouville at the Saumur Races for riding the horses Orphelin and Mishap.

Cartridge Arms

Although cartridges primed with percussion caps had been designed as early as the 1820s, the development of machine-made, self-contained metallic cartridges did not take place until some thirty years later. In the earliest versions, the interior base of the cartridge was covered with a fulminate of mercury paste. In later versions, this paste was spun into the edge or rim of the cartridge case. In both cases, however, ignition of the cartridge took place when the base or rim was struck sharply by a firing pin. Initially designed only for small caliber pistols, self-contained cartridges suitable for military uses—i.e. of larger caliber—were quickly developed for use during the Civil War.

While percussion cap revolvers and single-shot longarms remained the most commonly used firearms during that conflict, a number of cartridge repeating weapons were used with considerable effectiveness. For example, a soldier armed with a sixteen-shot Henry repeating rifle was, for all purposes, equal to sixteen soldiers armed with single-shot muzzle-loading muskets. In situations that could be decided by volume of fire, therefore, those troops equipped with repeating arms had a decided advantage. In addition, the

use of self-contained metallic cartridges made loading a much simpler and faster operation. Instead of the three operations necessary to load a percussion firearm—placing the black powder charge in the barrel or cylinder chamber, ramming home the bullet, and placing a cap on the nipple—there now was only one: chambering the cartridge in the barrel breech. Needless to say, cartridge firearms rapidly replaced those that used percussion caps.

Although the transition from the percussion to cartridge system occurred readily in Europe, where individual gunsmith shops still produced cartridge arms, the changeover in America took longer. Cost was the major problem, for although industrialization had simplified the process of manufacturing firearms, a considerable amount of money was needed to retool factories for the production of cartridge arms. Companies formed after the general introduction of cartridges had

a significant advantage over older firms. By 1870, however, the transition in America had been accomplished, and from this time forward cartridge arms of all different types dominated the market.

In the American West, the most commonly used cartridge arms were the Colt Model 1873 single-action army revolver (commonly referred to as either the "Peacemaker" or "Frontier Six-Shooter") and the Winchester Model 1866 or 1873 rifles. In time, thanks to a clever Winchester advertising slogan, the Winchester Model 1873 became known as "The Gun That Won The West." In actuality, the humble double-barrel shotgun probably deserves this title more, as homesteaders used countless thousands to provide game for their tables.

The 1890s saw the introduction of a new type of gunpowder. Smokeless powder—so named because it did not produce a cloud of white smoke when fired, as black powder did—offered

many advantages for firearms designers, most significantly the fact that a specific amount of powder now produced set pressures on a consistent basis. Therefore, they could design self-loading firearms operated by the recoil of a cartridge going off or the gas produced by the burning powder. The era of the semi-automatic and fully automatic firearm had arrived.

In recent years, attempts have been made to replace self-contained metallic cartridges with miniature rocket projectiles and caseless ammunition, in which the bullet is embedded in a moulded powder mixture that is fully combustible. So far these innovations have yet to see large-scale production.

True improvements do continue to be made in the design, reliability, and safety of firearms. Although some arms still superficially resemble those manufactured a century ago, internally they are far different. The quality of materials used in their construction is likewise far superior. What the future holds, no one can say, but based on the last five hundred years of gunmaking, new developments will probably be as revolutionary.

Air Guns

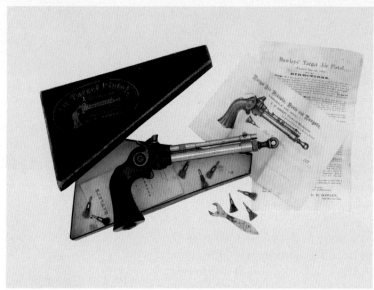

From the sixteenth century on, the development of firearms paralleled the creation of another type of projectile arm: the air gun. Today air guns are thought of primarily as BB type arms, but in their original form they were intended for hunting game.

Made in both single-shot and repeating forms, the air guns of the sixteenth, seventeenth, eighteenth, and early nineteenth centuries generally used reservoirs that could be filled with air by means of a pump quite similar to that used for pumping up bicycle tires. In some instances, the air reservoirs surrounded the barrel itself; in others, a ball-shaped reservoir was suspended from the piece or it was concealed within the shoulder stock.

Whatever the form of the air gun, contemporary records document that they were highly efficient, as well as silent. For example, Meriwether Lewis recorded in his diaries that the Lukens air rifle he took on his explorations of the American Northwest with William Clark could kill not only small game, but also deer.

By the mid-nineteenth century, air guns were primarily made for target shooting, and this remains their primary purpose today.

Combination Arms

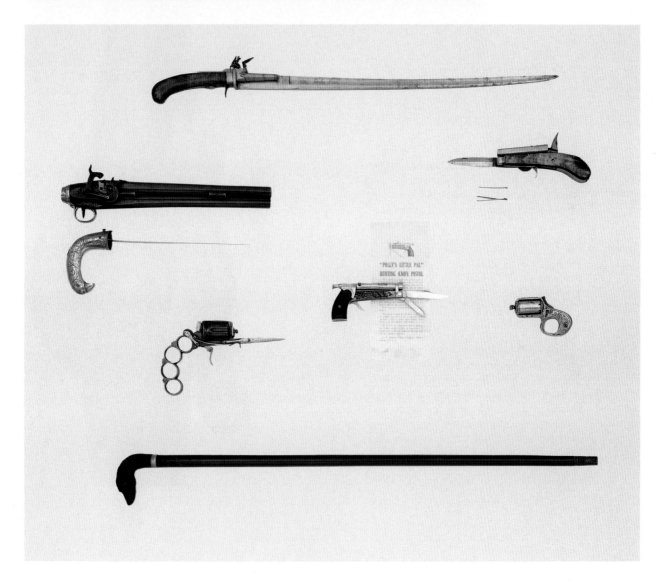

From almost the very beginning of the usage of firearms, gunmakers have combined them with other weapons to construct multiple-purpose pieces that may be best described as illustrating the adage: If at first you don't succeed, try, try again.

Early arms—built mainly upon polearms such as pikes, spears, and halberds—yielded by the eighteenth century to swords as the favored mounts. To a great extent, hunters used specially designed sword-pistols, as the sword was still the most widely accepted means of delivering the killing blow to wounded game. The attached pistol, however, provided insurance in case the hunter was not too skillful.

During the nineteenth century, pistols were mounted with daggers and brass knuckles. Despite their lethal appearance, for the most part such weapons were oddities designed for display rather than use. Those combined with pocket knives, however, did achieve wide use, as they were easily concealed.

63

▶

Cartridge Magazine Cover Plate
Belgian
Circa 1857
Signed: H. Genhard Breveté
Diameter 2 ¾″
In many respects, the care taken in the decoration
of this one element, on an otherwise absolutely plain
firearm, is representative of the restrained elegance
occasionally found on arms produced during the Second
Empire in France under the reign of Napoleon III.

▼

Repeating Cartridge Rifle
American
Circa 1854
Overall length: 43″
Barrel length: 23″
Caliber: .52
In 1854, the Smith & Wesson partnership of Norwich,
Connecticut, began production of a series of firearms
that used a lever-actuated sliding breech block and
hollow lead bullets filled with powder together with an
integral primer. This endeavor was not successful, and
all rights were purchased subsequently by Oliver F.
Winchester. In 1860, Benjamin Tyler Henry modified
the system for use with metallic cartridges and proved
the validity of the original design, for it evolved into the
Winchester rifle.

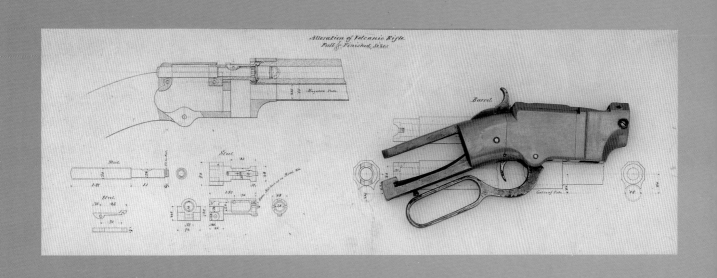

▲
Repeating Cartridge Rifle Receiver
American
Circa
1859-1860
Unsigned [New Haven Arms Company,
    New Haven, Connecticut]
Overall length: 7-13/16″
This receiver is the original model constructed by
Benjamin Tyler Henry to demonstrate the feasibility of
manufacturing repeating rifles using metallic cartridges.
The arm developed from this model was the renowned
Henry rifle, which in turn was modified to become the
Winchester rifle.

Prize Medal
Universal Exposition of 1867
Silver
Diameter: 2″
Although in dire economic straits after the Civil War,
the Spencer Repeating Rifle Company continued to
market its products aggressively. At the Universal
Exposition of 1867 in Paris, France, the company
received this silver medal for the excellence of
their arms.

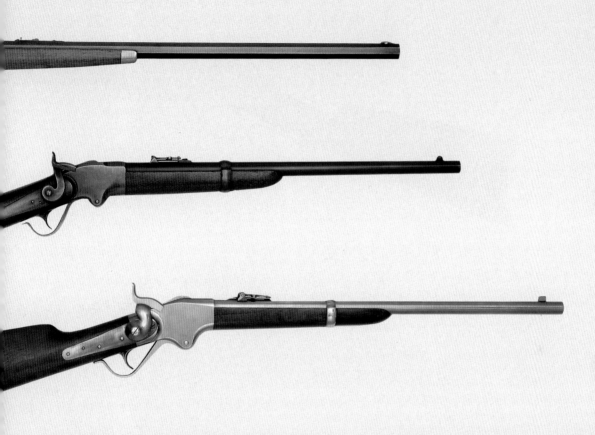

▲

Repeating Cartridge Rifles
American
Circa 1860
Maker: C.M. Spencer, Hartford, Connecticut
Overall Lengths 41″, 35¾″, 3¾″
Barrel Lengths 25⅝″, 19⅜″, 20″
Calibers .36, .41, .44
One of the first successful repeating cartridge rifles to
be produced in North America was that designed by
C.M. Spencer of Hartford, Connecticut. The three
prototypes here show the initial development of the
design from one suitable for sporting purposes to
one usable by the military. During the Civil War, the
federal government purchased 76,163 Spencer carbines
and rifles.

▶
Repeating Cartridge Rifle
American
Circa 1866-1867
Maker: The American Repeating Rifle Company,
Boston, Massachusetts
Overall length: 37¼″
Barrel length: 20¼″
Caliber: .46
Despite a general depression in the American arms
industry after the Civil War, some firms attempted
to introduce and market new firearms. One of these
enterprises, the American Repeating Rifle Company,
produced arms under patents granted to V. Fogerty.
Production, however, was severely limited and it is
unlikely that more than 50 specimens were made in
addition to the patent model shown here. In 1870, the
company went bankrupt and its assets were purchased
by the Winchester Repeating Arms Company.

◀

Repeating Cartridge Rifle
American
Circa 1863
Maker: New Haven Arms Company,
New Haven, Connecticut
Overall length: 43¼"
Barrel length: 24"
Caliber: .44
Loaned by Dr. Kenneth O. Leonard
Called "the rifle that could be loaded on Sunday and shot all week," the Henry rifle was one of the most sought-after military arms of the Civil War. While plain examples were much more common, engraved versions, such as the one illustrated here, were sold in considerable quantities to officers and civilians between 1862 and 1865.

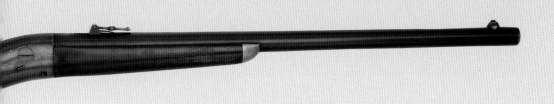

▲
Repeating Cartridge Rifle
American
Circa 1875
Maker: Winchester Repeating Arms Company,
    New Haven, Connecticut
Overall length: 43⅛″
Barrel length: 24⅜″
Caliber: .44
This sectionalized sample of the Winchester Model
1873 was constructed for display by the company
at the Centennial Exhibition held in Philadelphia,
Pennsylvania, in 1876. While primarily used to instruct
workmen on how a firearm was assembled and the
mechanics of its function, sectionalized samples
also proved to be excellent sales tools.

▲
Breech-Loading Cartridge Rifle
American
Circa 1878
Maker: Browning Brothers, Ogden, Utah
Overall length: 28″
Barrel length: 21⅜″
Caliber: .44
Bearing the serial number 1, this single-shot rifle made
by John M. Browning was the sample given to T.G.
Bennett of the Winchester Repeating Arms Company.

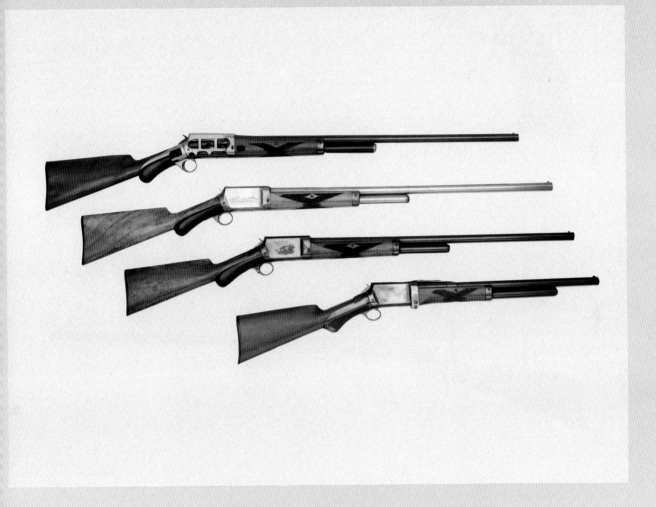

▲

Repeating Cartridge Shotguns
American
Circa 1893
Maker: The Burgess Gun Company
The above group of arms formed part of the display
mounted by the Burgess Gun Company at the World's
Columbian Exposition held in Chicago in 1893. As well
as illustrating the function and various styles of the
Burgess shotgun, the arms in the display also were
engraved with the various forms of decoration offered
by the company. In 1899, the Burgess Gun Company was
purchased by the Winchester Repeating Arms Company.

▲
Cartridge Target Pistol
American
Circa 1900
Maker: J. Stevens, Chicoppee Falls, Massachusetts
Overall length: 13″
Barrel length: 9⅝″
Caliber: .22
One of the most prolific manufacturers of firearms designed specifically for target shooting was the J. Stevens Company of Chicoppee Falls, Massachusetts. Characterized by long barrels, special adjustable sights, and well-formed grips, these target pistols were produced in quantity between 1890 and 1920.

▲
Breech-Loading Cartridge Rifle
American
Circa 1914
Maker: J. Stevens, Chicopee Falls, Massachusetts
Overall length: 47″
Barrel length: 29⅞″
Caliber: .32
The Stevens Company was one of the most prolific manufacturers of target rifles during the late nineteenth and early twentieth centuries. This quite plain example is typical of the majority of the arms the company produced.

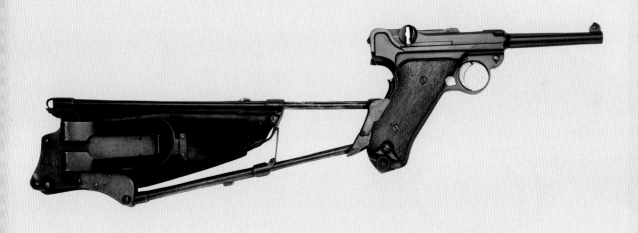

▲
Self-Loading Cartridge Rifle
American
Circa 1900
Maker: Winchester Repeating Arms Company,
New Haven, Connecticut
Overall length: 35⅞"
Barrel length: 17¾"
Caliber: .44
During the 1880s it was discovered that the recoil
produced by a cartridge being fired could be harnessed
to operate a firearms action. Thomas G. Bennett and
William Mason developed one of the first designs
for the Winchester Company that incorporated this
principle. Patented on March 18, 1902, this design was
never put into production.

▲
Self-Loading Pistol
German
Circa 1901
Maker: Deutsches Waffen und Munition Fabrik,
    Berlin, Germany
Overall length: 22½" (with stock)
Barrel length: 4½"
Caliber: 7.65mm
The pistols designed by Georg Luger are perhaps
the most recognizable modern self-loading pistols
ever made. Adopted for military use by a number of
European nations, they were quite popular in the United
States where some examples were fitted with a detach-
able combination shoulder stock and holster such as
those shown here.

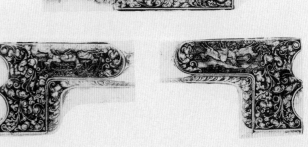

► Engraver's Pulls
American
Circa 1914
Unsigned [Rudolf J. Kornbrath]
"Pulls" are negative prints made by pressing rice paper into engraving that has been inked. These pulls are from the Rudolf J. Kornbrath Archives, and illustrate the engraving he executed on a Baker Gun Company Superba Grade trap gun.

▲ Breech-Loading Cartridge Shotgun
American
Circa 1918
Maker: Baker Gun Company
Overall length: 48½″
Barrel length: 32″
Caliber: 12 gauge
Although Baker trap guns were standard production arms, the three grades produced—the Sterling, Elite and Superba—were made up only on special order. Because of this, no two exactly like. This Elite Grade trap gun was engraved by one of the foremost twentieth-century engravers, Rudolf J. Kornbrath.

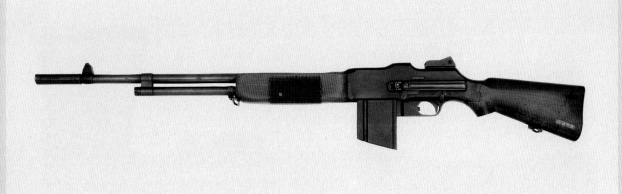

▲
Self-Loading Selective Fire Cartridge Rifle
American
Circa 1918
Maker: Winchester Repeating Arms Company,
New Haven, Connecticut
Overall length: 43¾"
Barrel length: 23¾"
Caliber: .30-06
The Browning Automatic Rifle designed by John M.
Browning was, and is, one of the finest light machine
guns ever made. Extensively used from World War I
through the Vietnam War, the B.A.R. has proven its
reliability and effectiveness worldwide.

◄
Self-Loading Cartridge Pistol
American
Circa 1918
Maker: Colt's Patent Fire Arms Manufacturing
    Company, Hartford, Connecticut
Overall length: 8¼"
Barrel length: 5"
Caliber: .45
In preparation for the Winchester Repeating Arms
Company to begin production of the Colt Model 1911
self-loading or semi-automatic pistol for the U.S.
government in 1918, the Colt Company sent a sec-
tionalized example (serial number C97756) to the
Winchester plant. Sectionalized firearms were used
by arms companies to familiarize plant personnel and
potential customers with designs, as well as for displays.

▲
Self-Loading Selective Fire Cartridge Rifle
American
Circa 1918
Maker: Winchester Repeating Arms Company,
    New Haven, Connecticut
Overall length: 45½″
Barrel length: 26″
Caliber: .341
This rifle, designed by T.C. Johnson, can be accurately
described as the first assault rifle ever to have been
made. Using a short, small-caliber cartridge, this piece
was light enough to be carried easily by an infantryman,
and, due to its twin magazine, could deliver forty
rounds of fire without reloading. By pressing the trigger
within the trigger guard, the rifle fired one cartridge at
a time. However, when the extension below the trigger
guard was pulled, pressure on the trigger caused the
rifle to fire automatically.

▶
Self-Loading Cartridge Rifles
American
Circa 1941-1942
Maker: Winchester Repeating Arms Company,
New Haven, Connecticut
Overall lengths: 35⅛″, 35⅜″, 35⅝″
Barrel lengths: 17¾″, 17⅞″, 17⅞″
Calibers: .30
One of the most successful and speedy firearms develop-
ment programs ever initiated involved the designing of
the U.S. M-1 carbine. The first prototype (top) was built
in thirteen days; the perfected example (middle) was
made approximately thirty days later. As the first pro-
duction example (bottom) demonstrates, little change
took place between the beginning of the project and
its completion.

▼
Self-Loading Rocket Launcher
American
Circa 1965
Maker: MAB Associates
Overall length: 33½"
Barrel length: 16½"
Caliber: 13mm
The Gyrojet system (this example is a Mark I Model B carbine) does not use cartridges of the normal type. Rather, it fires projectiles that are miniature rockets. The barrel is merely a tube in which the projectile accelerates and assumes a stable spin. Despite the promise this system showed, it was not manufactured in quantity.

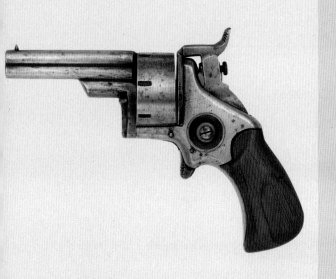

◄
Cartridge Revolver
American
Circa 1863
Unsigned [Jacob Rupertus, Philadelphia, Pennsylvania]
Overall length: 7"
Barrel length: 3"
Caliber: .20
In an attempt to increase the capabilities of the revolving cylinder system, Jacob Rupertus designed a revolver whose cylinder was bored with two concentric rings of cartridge chambers. By using two vertically mounted barrels, this pistol could deliver fourteen rounds in two-shot volleys or, by adjusting the hammer, singly by either the upper or lower barrel.

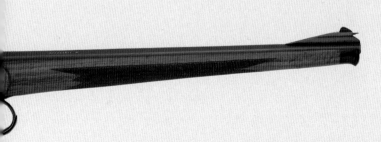

Cartridge Repeating Pistol
French
Circa 1865
Signed: J. Jarre, Paris, France
Overall length: 9¾″
Barrel length: 4¼″
Caliber: .36
Among the many attempts to produce effective revolvers in the 1850s, Jarre's patent was one of the more unusual.

Magazine Cartridge Pistol
French
Circa 1855
Signed: M.N. Colleye, Paris, France
Overall length: 9½″
Barrel length: 4″
Caliber: .36
The action of pulling the trigger on this pistol automatically caused the vertical bar containing the cartridge chambers to rise, thus bringing fresh rounds into firing position. Despite its impracticality, numerous examples of this system were made and sold.

Cartridge Target Pistol
German
Circa 1930
Maker: H. Scherping, Hanover, Germany
Overall length: 21″
Barrel length: 14½″
Caliber: .22
Gift of Stans African Hall, Museum of York County,
    Rock Hill, South Carolina
The form of this target pistol is unusual in that the forestock is patterned after that normally encountered on sporting carbines—i.e., the wood extends to the muzzle.

CODY FIREARMS MUSEUM MEMBERSHIPS

Take advantage of an opportunity to celebrate America's finest firearms museum. The Buffalo Bill Historical Center offers three levels of memberships designed to support the Cody Firearms Museum.

For information on making these new membership commitments, contact the membership office of the Historical Center at P.O. Box 1000, Cody, Wyoming 82414 or (307) 587-4771.